ONLY FOOLS AND BOSSES
Neglect Respect

The Bosses' Guide
to Gaining Respect

Martin Fisher

ISBN No: 978-1-903680-09-4
published by Denny Publishing
November 2010
www.dennypublishing.co.uk

ONLY FOOLS AND BOSSES
Neglect Respect
**The Bosses' Guide
to Gaining Respect**
First published in 2010
© Martin Fisher

The Bosses' Guide to Gaining Respect

CONTENTS

Foreword v

Biography ix

Introduction xiii

réspĕct′¹, n.

FOREWORD

RESPECT has become an abused word in our society. It is devalued by young people demanding it, management expecting it and fools who crave it – whatever it is.

Some new leadership research hit the press in September 2010. Professor Alex Higman and Dr Kim Peters, psychologists at Exeter University, completed a yearlong study looking at what makes a great leader. The results have surprised many - not the author - in that it is bosses who stay in touch with their followers and support those who they lead. This clashes with conventional ideas that the best leaders were driven individuals with domineering personalities.

They have recognised a number of traits that lead to successful leaders amongst which are being sensitive to followers, being positive and inspirational and treating followers with RESPECT. Other factors included meeting staff expectations and avoiding arrogance. They also identified that leaders fall from grace when instead of recognising that their success depends on keeping a good relationship with their followers they begin to believe their own hype and their decline in popularity begins.

One of the greatest leaders of all time, Sir Earnest Shackleton, the Antarctic explorer exemplifies almost every attribute of successful leadership. In my opinion the best book ever written on leadership, 'Shackleton's Way' by Morrell and Capparell, clearly demonstrates the unique power of respect.

Martin Fisher's book will become a must read for every manager and aspiring leader. Now I have to confess that in writing this preface I am wearing two hats, the hat of the publisher and that of the reviewer.

My Reviewer's Hat

Over the years I have amassed quite a collection of business books, although sadly many appealed from the title and promised content. I really wanted and, in many cases, needed the help and guidance that appeared to be offered. I also have to confess that so many were dipped into but then left unread - why? Well in all honesty, they were hard work. Small print, long paragraphs, five or six words where two would suffice.

'Only Fools and Bosses' has all of the ticks in all of the right boxes for me. Martin Fisher has a wealth of practical experience and he has written a superb, practical and useable piece of work. This book is filled with common sense (unusual today where people are too busy to be confused with common sense). It is a delight. It is so easy to read and I really hope and believe it will become a best seller for him. If ever a subject needed addressing, supported with the all important HOW TO'S this book delivers.

Publisher's Hat

We are approached by many authors and very occasionally a manuscript arrives that really gets us excited. Martin Fisher not only is an authority on this subject, but he provides and delivers workshops, lectures and seminars to a wide variety of audiences. This book is the right size for people who are busy and are suffering from information overload. We are delighted to say that 'Only Fools and Bosses' carries our full guarantee of satisfaction. I hope that you enjoy it and recommend it to your contacts.

Richard Denny

respect'¹, n.

MARTIN FISHER

MARTIN Fisher left school with 4 A levels electing not to go on to further education. He joined a major insurance company on their accelerated development scheme and became the youngest new business inspector in the country at the age of 20. While there he achieved his first professional qualification (Associate of the Chartered Insurance Institute). He won a number of awards for exam performance and was part of a national winning quiz team for his local Insurance Institute. Whilst working in this role an Insurance Broker headhunted him into a directorship responsible for developing the general insurance side of the business which he did for 10 years, moving the company from a mainly life and pensions business to a substantial general insurance business which still thrives today.

During this period Martin was a Special Constable in Watford and achieved successive promotions to head up that division. He found this an invaluable period in his life bringing him into contact with areas that most are protected from in day to day living. During this period Martin won a commendation for the way he and a regular Police Officer dealt with a very large scale disturbance in the town centre while waiting (what seemed like hours!) for help to arrive. The thing that Martin takes most from this period is the support of colleagues. The Police, like any other organisation, has people who like each other, don't like each other or even really hate each other. But, when the chips are down and a fellow officer needs help nothing gets in the way, whether that officer is your best buddy or your worst enemy. If only we could take that loyalty into the office situation.

In 1989 Martin took a trial flying lesson in a light aircraft and was immediately hooked! After just 5 hours flying he decided he could go all the way and qualify commercially. Even just a private license is a minimum of 40 hours flying time with a commercial requiring 700 hours! He sold his share of the business to fund the high cost of commercial qualification. The next 15 months was spent flying, going on training courses and, when the weather was bad, studying for exams. He spent a month flying in the USA when the weather was too bad to fly in the UK and has threatened to publish the extensive diary he wrote while flying around Florida. A cross between a flying manual and an episode of *Men Behaving Badly*! Dodgy nightclubs, alligators on the runway and landing at a known drugs courier's airfield are just some of the things that happened in that month.

It was at Bournemouth Airport that Martin completed his final commercial flying test to qualify in 1990. The time taken, 15 months, is one of the fastest ever achieved through the 'self starter' route. Martin realised that his timing wasn't perfect when on the very day he qualified the local major airline in Bedfordshire, near to where he lived, made 90 pilots redundant due to the recession. Being resourceful he undertook a number of jobs and tasks to make sure the mortgage was paid on time over the next few months - (don't ask him about selling timeshare!)

When it became obvious that the flying world would take many years to recover and with hundreds, if not thousands, of pilots with 'jet hours' still seeking work there was unlikely to be any opportunities for 'wet behind the ears' newly qualified pilots, he decided to get back into what he was best qualified in. Martin joined a major High Street Bank in 1992 as a Financial Services Adviser before moving to a marketing role where he spent two years making presentations to groups of customers and staff - presenting to literally thousands of people from Truro to Edinburgh.

He then moved on to head up the Internal Training Team responsible for all the major departments of the Financial Services area of the bank. While Martin was training manager he helped the bank achieve the prestigious Investors in People Award.

Subsequently Martin went on to run the sales management function of the Financial Services team responsible for the high net worth customers of the bank. During that time he furthered his professional qualifications becoming a Fellow of the Chartered Insurance Institute and achieving DipPFS. Part of his remit was to be responsible for high performer awards events and after 13 years Martin decided it was time to go it alone so set up Clifford Solutions Ltd, a conference management and organisation company.

Their clients are many and varied, including some financial services organisations as well as franchises, trade bodies and manufacturers/distributers. Martin has also created a new website for the Polish community in the Southampton area and undertakes Financial Services consultancy work.

Outside of work Martin is married, is a keen golfer, an even keener Watford FC supporter and is kept busy by his 8 year old son. His attitude is that there are things in life you can do nothing about, world recessions and the like, so you have to get out there and make things happen for yourself. As demonstrated by his abortive flying career, it is far better for you to try things and maybe not succeed for whatever reason, than to spend life wishing you had tried.

What qualifies him to write about and speak on the subject of respect? Martin has worked with many senior managers in both multi-national and local organisations. He has managed teams varying from junior staff to experienced managers. Martin has looked at the wealth of experience he has and has identified what helps a manager gain respect. All of the situations he describes have really happened - some to Martin, some to others he knows and he has admitted to being the (occasional) perpetrator of some of the less successful respect strategies. What he has established is that the managers who get the real 'extra mile' from their teams succeed by gaining respect - a much more powerful motivator than fear, which sadly many think is the key to success.

These are real situations, real people, and real strategies to help get the most out of real teams.

INTRODUCTION

THE aim of this short, easy-to-read reference guide is simple.

Respect! Think about how many bosses you have respected? Some a lot, some a little and some not at all? The rules of respect are pretty simple, they don't guarantee everyone will like you but they will show you respect - at the very least more than before you read this guide (assuming you take on board the points of course!).

What is respect? The dictionary defines it as; To feel or show deferential regard for; esteem./A feeling of appreciative, often deferential regard; esteem./The state of being regarded with honour or esteem.

Microsoft 'Word' Thesaurus shows (as Microsoft appears to have taken over the world), among others, words relating to respect; *Admiration, High opinion, Deference, Esteem, Reverence, Look up to, Value, Think a lot of*

I don't think anyone could argue with these definitions.

Yes, it is possible to respect someone you don't like, someone you don't agree with, BUT respect helps break down those barriers. A lot of people respected Margaret Thatcher - possibly a few less liked her!

Why bother with gaining respect - you can get the job done by your position. Yes, you can get *A* job done, but probably not **the** best job done. What are the advantages of gaining respect?

Self esteem - you can hold your head high.

Loyalty - how often do you need a favour? A bit of extra work when there is no overtime available, a hand with a job that has to be completed in unsocial hours.

A good reputation - good staff will want to work for you.

If you have to get 'tough' with someone it will be easier. That person is more likely to take it from someone who they respect. Even if they don't accept what you say, a serious situation is unlikely to destabilise the team to the same extent if they respect the boss. You will gain respect by dealing with problems in the team - no one likes a passenger.

Bottom line - more output from the team which will reflect on you.

Research published early in 2008 for Investors in People clearly shows the link between effective people management and business success. The two year study indicates that companies with effective people management showed higher profits per employee, higher profit margins and higher productivity.

What is the link between effective people management and respect? Think about it. Think about the managers you have respected - were they more effective as people managers than those you didn't? I think so.

So if we agree that respect is important, if not vital, to achieving the maximum from your team, how do you achieve it? There are three things you have to commit to, to make any of the 'tips' in this guide work - Time, Prioritisation and Consistency. Gaining respect is easy - losing it is even easier.

You need to take the time to deal with these issues correctly. It may seem like a lot of time but it WILL pay dividends. Footballer's pre- season training is hard but they get the benefit later on. If you don't give time to these issues you will lose respect, you will lose output and you will find it harder to take the team with you.

Priorities are vital. What are yours? Yes an external customer will take priority and you should build a culture that recognises that. It is your customers who 'pay the wages'. However after that your main priority is YOUR team. For you to be recognised, for you to get the promotion you want, for you to succeed in your goals, you need your team with you.

Consistency is vital. One of the hardest things to do is to work with someone who is inconsistent. You need to make sure that your team knows what is expected, that you treat everyone fairly and that you react the same to a given set of circumstances. Think about how you can be seen to be consistent when you read the various chapters. We hear the phrase 'moody' - that often describes someone who is inconsistent. It makes respect harder to achieve.

Respect works in the same way as the good news bad news ratio. If you do something well that customer will probably tell one person. If you do it badly they will tell 10. Respect is similar in that it is ten times easier to lose than to gain. Think about that when you see yourself in some of the following chapters.

Understand what respect is. 'My team respects me because of the hours I work.' Ummmm do they? Or do they think you are a bit sad with no other life? Do they laugh at your continual 4.00am emails? I can't remember the last time I heard, 'I really respect him/her as they sat up until 4.00am sending me emails…'

An old boss of mine once sent me an email at 7.00pm on a Saturday asking for information by 8.30 Monday morning. Sadly I did see it but responded on Tuesday anyway to make a point! Did I respect him? No I thought he had a cheek even expecting me to see his note before 8.30 Monday morning. (Actually he never mentioned how late the information was – must have been really important – not.)

So much of respect is basic courtesy and manners – so why do bosses need this guide at all? Because for some reason otherwise intelligent people leave basic courtesy and manners in the car park with the company car when they get to work. The person who uses 'please' and 'thank you' in all forms of life can mysteriously forget them at work – the place where you spend over half your waking hours in the week. (Of course some never use 'please' or 'thank you' inside or outside work – this guide may not be enough for them…)

The methods they use to get things done outside work seem to go by the wayside in the office/factory etc.

We have all heard 'They are scary – but they get things done' – but how much more would they get done by having the team on side? A CEO of a major international company I used to be involved with 'got things done' by making life very unpleasant for everyone, including senior managers, around him (one of his most senior direct reports resigned because, 'I have got to my position after 30 years of hard work and have no wish to come to work to be shouted at every day.').

The CEO had to go to brief Government treasury ministers every so often - the brief from his team was never as thorough as the brief given to his well respected predecessor. If he got a hard time at the Treasury it was worth the fall out back at the office! A lack of respect for him made the pain worthwhile. His predecessor could have run over a cliff lemming like and everyone would have run over with him. If this guy had run over the cliff there would be a lot of people watching and waving.

People are your most valuable commodity - bar none. How much more does a manager get from a team that respect them rather than a team that doesn't? My guess is in excess of 30% - do you want another 30%?

This book is practical - there aren't hundreds of 'models' that explain behaviours. There are good practical tips. There are plenty of REAL examples (**all** examples in this book are real). Where do they come from? They come from 30 years of having been a victim (and dare I say a perpetrator at times) of all of the situations covered. If anyone who manages people can honestly say they have never been guilty of any of the practices (offences?) outlined in this book then congratulations - or have you really looked in the mirror?

If, like most people, and 100% of the good managers, you are aware of your shortcomings then well done - recognising that you have shortcomings is the start to get things right and gaining or increasing the respect you have from your team. Like most guides of any kind it is almost impossible to take on 100% of the ideas mentioned - little and often is a good way to improve. Look at the ideas, apply them to yourself as you feel comfortable. Then re-read and move another step forward. If you think you need this book you will benefit greatly - if you think you don't need it - you will benefit enormously! But, only if you are open minded and can accept that we are not all perfect.

Let's start with the real stuff - how do we gain respect?

The ABC of this is all down to **YOU**. Gaining respect is about;

YOUR Actions

YOUR Business culture

YOUR Communication

There is a 'U' as well but that doesn't fit with an ABC !

YOUR Understanding.

Therefore this book is divided into chapters based on the 4 'Yours'. We have left the 'A' for Action section until last as that is the one you will need in the front of your mind the most. We will start with the Communication section moving through to Understanding before Business Culture and Actions - CUBA!

COMMUNICATION

In this section we will look at the various communication opportunities there are to gain, or lose, respect.

1 to 1s

The description that came in a few years ago to describe a meeting of two people - where would we be without people inventing a name for a type of meeting that has gone on for hundreds of years? Oh well…

Anyway, 1 to 1s. What happens? You make an appointment to speak to someone who sits 3m from you and who you see every day. It will be:

a) Postponed and re-scheduled (usually by the boss),

b) Late (usually thanks to the boss),

Sorry, but these are the unwritten rules that apply. Maybe a little respect can be gained by ignoring a) and b) above and being on time on the date in question? Yes sometimes urgent and/or important things come up. BUT 90% of postponements and late meetings are the result of poor diary management or lack of respect to the team member. X is far more important than you, I didn't bother to check what time because it was only you…

Then what happens? The boss spends the whole time telling the other party what he or she wants, gets interrupted by phone calls (which they take), BlackBerry emails which they read at 3 minute intervals, and then says 'Sorry I have another meeting so we can catch up with the rest another day.' The rest being the fact that you have an idea to make the company millions, you have a serious issue out of work, your husband/wife has left you to run off with a demented axe murderer (this implies some axe murderers are not demented - discuss?), you are going on holiday that afternoon never to come back etc. etc. etc. This is not David Brent from *'The Office'*. This is real!

The answer is simple. Just be there when you say where you say. My 8 year old is quite good at telling the time – I have had plenty of bosses who, although a little older, are not so good. Perhaps there is a market for a 'When the big hand is on the…' book in business – I'll mention that to my publisher.

DO NOT BE LATE. 99.78% of all people late for meetings have no real reason except their inability to manage their own time (the 99.78% is a made up figure but is VERY close to the truth). LATE equals a lack of respect – the employee sits and wastes 10 minutes waiting for you – is their time less valuable than yours? Should your boss bill YOU for the wasted company time YOU caused?

Example: A company of 1,000 people - there are 20 1 to 1s a day. Each is delayed by 20 minutes because someone is late - that's 800 minutes straight away of completely wasted company time. How much is that worth…? 4000 minutes a week, 17,200 minutes a month, 208,400 minutes a year - hang on that's an extra employee or two! In this example we have wasted the time of 2 full time employees hanging around for meetings. Get an increase in headcount for zero cost!

Your only priority in a 1 to 1 is the person you are having the 1 to 1 with. How many times have you been in a meeting and had the other person take phone calls, read messages on the BlackBerry etc. The ONLY excuse is if the subject matter is directly related to the subject you are talking about.

Example: you are trying to get your employee on a training course and you phone for an update. Taking other calls shows a lack of respect.

Make a point of turning your phone/BlackBerry off – it gives a very powerful message – 'My meeting with you is important and I don't want to be interrupted'. Caution – the first time you do this after reading this book after months/years of taking calls the employee will be scared senseless and think they are going to be sacked or similar – remember that only by being consistent in how you deal with these matters will people know where they stand.

The overall point about 1 to 1s? Try not to have many! If you deal with issues as they arrive and are open to approach you won't need nearly so many 1 to 1s. You both know exactly where you are all of the time. When one of my team said to me 'I have just found out in a 1 to 1 XXX has a serious issue regarding YYY which will impact what we are doing' I wanted to know why we didn't know two weeks previously when the issue had arisen. The answer was that they hadn't had a 1 to 1 – they worked 15m apart!

1 to 1s that do happen should therefore be:

■ **Focused**

■ **Agenda driven**

■ **Related to work issues pertaining to the employee**

■ **Related to personal development of the employee**

■ **A catch up on what is important for that person**

And not a forum for surprises.

Be consistent. We've all heard, 'She's/he's been on a course I see, don't worry it will all go back to normal soon enough…' . Consistency is about making those changes stick – it will be the new you again in 6 months and 6 years not for just 6 minutes.

TIP If you are the boss and you are late (on an exceptional occasion - not the norm) it is your part of the meeting that should be cut down not other peoples'.

Don't make appointments

Do you make an appointment whenever you want to tell someone in your team something - or even do you make the appointment through your secretary to do the same? Please try not to. Encourage a culture where issues get dealt with straight away. This encourages business efficiency and makes for a much more open and engaging atmosphere. Yes, do have team meetings to get everyone together and do have 1 to 1s to discuss individual issues, appraisals and the like. BUT if you have something to tell someone, good, bad or indifferent, do it there and then (not in front of others if it is personal or a criticism).

In terms of team meetings and communication what about morning meetings (these have been called prayer meetings in some quarters - a term I would resist at all costs - far too many unnecessary connotations - mixed religions and no religion in the workplace etc.). They should be very short and focused on the real and current issues that help everyone do their job.

Effective communication = respect. Try it, it does.

One of the best ways to lose respect is to communicate badly, late or not at all. How can you respect a boss who doesn't let you know what is going on? Some bosses think they know best when it comes to holding back information. Companies spend thousands employing communication teams and then a manager (in middle management usually) decides that his or her team do not need to know that particular piece of information so they won't pass it on. When the team finds out what is happening respect falls away.

Make time to communicate. Have the weekly/daily get together but don't forget that is not your only communication vehicle. It is your job to prioritise how and when communication happens from the casual conversation to a formal company announcement.

Be consistent. Your team will know when they will hear about different things. They won't be chasing you for information and will feel confident in what they do knowing they always have the information they need when they need it.

TIP With the increase in working at remote locations or from home make sure that out of sight is not out of mind. With the technology available there is no excuse for a lack of communication even if you are 500 miles apart - Alexander Graham Bell was a very clever chap.

Communicate effectively

Communication is key to respect as we have already seen. But it has to be effective communication. Whether it is daily meetings, 1 to 1s, appraisals or informal communication it has to be effective. What is effective? The simplest definition is that both parties understand the same thing about the subject matter in question. That sounds easy doesn't it? Think back to the times when you have done one thing but your boss was expecting something slightly different. Think back to when one of your team has done something slightly different to what you were expecting. Both occurrences will have happened because the communication was not effective.

Example: I joined a team and the boss was about to go on holiday. He briefed me and a colleague who had worked with him for several months on what he wanted us to do while he was away. I hadn't got a clue what he was talking about but sat there in the knowledge that my colleague would know and I could pick his brains later. He, on the other hand, was sitting there thinking what is this all about? He thought it must be something the boss had already mentioned to me and he could pick up with me later.

Result? Neither of us knew what we were supposed to do and the boss went away for 2 weeks!

When he got back we had to confess. His reaction? Great, he didn't apportion any blame (see Blame Culture) we all agreed how we would communicate in future and that we would challenge him when we did not understand, or disagreed with what he was saying. We held this boss in high regard and we got on with what we should have done while he was away with some gusto so we didn't let him down.

Make sure you create the time to make sure what you think has been communicated has been. Ask questions, have two way discussions – not tell sessions.

Communication has to be a priority. You cannot expect to get a good job done if you don't communicate effectively. You will lose respect when people do work for you and you continually say 'That's not what I wanted/not what I meant...'

TIP Test your communications at every opportunity. 'Have I made myself clear?' (not in a threatening way). 'What do you understand as the requirement?' Ask questions to test their understanding 'So how do you think this will work?'. How does your team want you to communicate? Your idea of perfect communication might not be theirs.

Remember the bosses you have respected? I would lay money on the fact that they were effective communicators.

What's in a word?

Ah, the touchy subject of Business language (I've heard it called worse). What do we mean? There are hundreds of examples of words and phrases that have been invented for very simple things so as to sound different and important.

Example: we need to get the outstanding items actioned. Or how about we need to get the outstanding items done? It is totally impossible to be in business and not be responsible for some Business BS (as it is otherwise known) but by being conscious of it you can reduce it to a level where people notice that you are not full of BBS - respect increases.

Some managers are so fluent in BBS that they can't speak any other language. Home life must be very interesting, 'Hello darling, hopefully we are on the same page for our refuel, so let's touch base over dinner and hope the TV ticks all the boxes…'

Those of you who remember the TV programme in the 90's *'Drop the Dead Donkey'* will remember that the character Gus was the absolute master of Business BS - if you can get hold of the DVDs they are hilarious and well worth watching. You can also find 'Gus-isms' on the internet.

Have you ever heard the phrase 'I respect his/her straight talking'? I guess we all have and you will find that the straight talker uses less BBS than others who are not thought of as such.

Let's look at some examples

BBS	PLAIN ENGLISH
Singing from the same hymn sheet Being on the same page	Offering a consistent / the same view
Low hanging fruit	Quick win/easy items
Paradigm shift	Change in thinking ('The lady is not for paradigm shifts' may not have sounded as good from Mrs Thatcher!)
Resources	People
Touch base	Speak
Downsizing	Reducing
Ball Park	Approximately
Repositioning	Changing
Revisit	Have another look at
Show stopper	Critical item
Ticks all the boxes	Meets all the requirements
I hear what you say	No
But with respect	You are completely wrong, you idiot!

Don't forget it's not just Business BS, but other use of language can cause confusion. One of the communication managers I worked with was very intelligent, privately educated and had a first class degree from a top university. She put together an 'inspirational' DVD with music and images to show at a conference. The words that appeared at the end of the DVD to inspire were 'Carpe Diem' - the Latin phrase which is translated as 'Seize the day'.

What percentage of her audience had studied Latin (as she had) - 1%? A good few knew the phrase from general knowledge but a high proportion had no idea what it meant - the impact of an otherwise excellent DVD was lost on them. Understand your audience! What was wrong in this case with using the English words?

I worked for one boss who was the 'plainest speaker' I have ever come across. He was totally unable to take part in Business BS – how refreshing! At one annual objective setting meeting (while I ran a sales management function) he said, 'You only have one objective - get rid of XXXXXX'. He had a real problem with one very awkward member of the team who successive managers had tried to move on without success. Due to luck and circumstance I achieved that by the April and asked if I could go home for the rest of the year. There was an equally succinct plain English reply...

TIP Use Blue Sky ideas that are outside the box to make sure everyone is on the same page. Get resources to pull together in a forward thinking paradigm so you can pool your brain spaces into a centre of excellence. Make sure you are a team player and touch base regularly. Above all grab the low hanging fruit and meet the team offline to achieve collective megathrust. Simple.

Chairing meetings

Anyone can do that can't they? Yes they can. But not always well. We have all been to meetings where the chairman is completely disorganised, people are late turning up, negatives are not discussed (one of NASA's worst accidents happened because their culture did not let people express anything considered as negative or of concern), the chairman 'hogs' the whole meeting and no one else gets involved, the meeting drags on so that it can hit its published end time and so on.

Meetings are, like emails, an incredibly effective communication medium or a waste of a lot of people's time and effort. If you are the chairman it is for you to make sure that they fall into the effective camp rather than the waste of time one. Some simple research in every company will show you that meetings start late. If there are 12 people kept waiting by a chairman who is 20 minutes late that is 240 minutes of completely wasted time – that is over half a day's worth of waste. A 10 person meeting that goes on for half an hour too long wastes 5 hours of valuable work time. An often witnessed extreme is a 20 person meeting starting 20 minutes late and going for ½ hour more than is necessary = over 2 man days wasted! How much work could you do in two days?

What are the rules of running a good meeting? Well some of the more simple ones are:

■ **That any meeting should have a start and a MAXIMUM end time.** We will finish by XX whatever happens.

■ **Try to avoid having AOB.** This is usually the chance for everyone to 'get things off their chest' and leave the meeting on a negative note. Ask for all items to be put on the agenda beforehand.

■ **Be upfront with known negatives** – that way you can deal with them, put them to one side and move on. Do not ignore them.

■ **Encourage contribution.** Expect people to contribute and expect them to be prepared.

■ **Do not ridicule ideas in a meeting** – this will instantly kill any creativity, and respect for you. Some of the greatest inventions ever produced sounded completely mad when first mentioned. In fact thinking about it most great inventions probably sounded mad at first hearing.

TIP For general meetings that you are running - start on time whether everyone is there or not. They will get the message soon enough when decisions are made and people missed them as they were late. (It's actually quite fun starting a meeting on your own and then seeing people's faces as they come in!) People will come to learn that you do start on time, you do not waste people's time and your respect will grow.

Email

For those of us that were at work 20 years ago how on earth did we communicate without email? It seems impossible - we had to speak to people face to face, we had to phone people or send a pigeon with a message - scary!

Email is one of the great inventions of our time but causes us stress and communication issues and a lack of respect when not used properly - which is a considerable percentage of the time. Two of the main uses of email are backside covering 'but I copied you in on that email 6 weeks ago' (along with the other 800 I sent you) and avoiding having to speak to people. Actually, I guess there is a third - 'a badge of honour'. 'I got 8,000 emails while I was on a two day holiday'. 'Is that all? I had 10,000 before breakfast on Christmas Day!' 'You were lucky, I had 100,000 emails that had to be read before work...' When appraisals are conducted based on email traffic there will be some significant beneficiaries.

Some managers rely on email as their main management tool. Email replaces face to face contact and phone calls. You cannot be an effective manager if you sit in your enclosed space and communicate by email. You won't get respect. I used to work with a guy who had the same amount of respect for the boss as I did - zero. He used to blind copy me in to their email arguments, rants and general communication for fun. It was hilarious! The manager was actually emailing in 'argument' form when the guy I worked with sat 5m away from him. Sad but true.

Email is a fantastic tool, BUT:

■ It should never be the tool to carry any sort of negative message to someone (there are loads of stories of redundancies and sackings by email).

■ It really shouldn't be used to say thank you. A personal note is always more powerful than an email. An email is better than nothing but think about whether it is the right way.

■ It is not a management tool - it is a communication tool.

■ It should not replace actually speaking to people. It is not quicker - we all see 'arguments' about points of fact via several back and forth emails. Why not pick up the phone, or walk round the corner to negotiate? Managers are paid serious amounts of money to be one fingered typists - use the skills you are good at negotiation and communication - one email to summarise the agreement - job done!

■ It should never be used as a backside covering mechanism. Even worse when you try to 'hide' the email amongst other correspondence. Remember the case of the Government secretary trying to get an unpopular decision through while 9/11 was unfolding? They thought no-one would notice!

TIP Think. Can I actually speak to someone rather than email?

Theft of Intellectual Property

That title made you look didn't it? What do I mean? We all know managers who never acknowledge the true 'author' of work they put out as their own. It is a fine line to follow - if you acknowledge everything as someone else's why do they need you? BUT, it is good for the individual and you to show how you have developed the team to acknowledge input from people. 'I am pleased to circulate the report as requested. John and Mary have done an excellent job in highlighting the issues which are shown on the attached.' John and Mary get good credit - your name is on the paper - win, win!

Don't blatantly regurgitate someone else's work as yours - if that's all you do why do they need you? It is incredibly annoying and definitely causes a loss of respect when the boss says here is my report and takes all the credit with no acknowledgement. Do you know how upsetting it is when you see the boss get a reward for a piece of work that you did with no acknowledgement? I bet you have had this happen to you when your boss has claimed your work as their own, It doesn't make you feel good.

The old public school system of fagging worked on the basis that prefects give the younger pupils a very hard time on the basis that when the youngsters get older they will do the same to the new younger intake. Pathetic! If business works in this way we never deal with the real issues - and it does. Just because the boss 'steals' your work that is no excuse to do the same to those under you.

However if the work is poor you can bet your bottom dollar that the lords and masters find out who did it pretty quickly.......'Ah yes sorry, that information came from George, I'll make sure he knows the impact of the incorrect information blah, blah, blah' signed yours Mr Teflon-Desk. (See Blame section).

If it's great it's mine – if it's poor it's yours!

Take pride in the work that your team does – it is through your guidance and encouragement that they do it. You will gain respect when people know that their good work is attributed to them

When is it best to 're-badge' work and when to just send it on? Learn about your audience and respond accordingly. Take your team with you.

TIP People thrive on confidence – if someone has done a great piece of work make sure people know about it. You will get them going the extra mile next time.

Share the vision – don't be a mushroom farmer!

One of the reasons a team may lack respect in a boss is where they are treated like mushrooms – kept in the dark and fed bull-xxxx. Where you find people who respect a boss you will usually find a boss who shares ideas and visions – the team know what they are all aiming at. You might think this is obvious but there are countless examples where teams do what they are told with no idea as to what they are trying to achieve.

It wouldn't make much sense if at the 2012 Olympics in London, runners were told – sorry can't tell you how far you will be running or in what direction but, 'On your marks…'. Maybe they would perform better if they knew it was a 10,000 metre race and would be held in an anti-clockwise direction around the 400m track.

We expect people to commit themselves to a role/job sometimes without telling them what event they are in let alone the distance. Do they run, throw or jump? (Some bosses just like their team to jump of course - only question required 'How high?').

Recent research highlighted that, within a high profile section of a major high street bank, none of the team 'at the coal face' seeing customers had the slightest idea what the business vision was. A survey of the internal team would unfortunately have come up with the same finding. How much respect is lost by not being even aware of where the boss and the company are going? Yes some people just want to turn up at 9.00, do their job and go home at 5.00 without getting involved in visions and strategies. But isn't that their choice? Perhaps not one for you to make on their behalf.

Yes things change, goals and visions evolve. But take people with you and they will respect that much more than not be-ing involved. You never know the next great vision might just come from them... I quote a former Sales Director I worked with - 'Everyone comes with a free brain.'

Time spent involving the team in visions and goals will pay dividends in terms of their respect for you as a boss and may just give you the best ideas 'you' have ever had. Don't let your team hear through the back door things that you should have communicated direct.

TIP Use team members to increase your 'visionary' brain power by a factor equal to the number in the team!

The 'R' word

Ah, the Redundancy word. We have to face the fact that in the present financial climate many businesses face the tough deci-sion to have to lay off staff. How do you communicate that and maintain respect? Actually you can go through this process and maintain or improve respect. If you go to the chapter on 'What drives people' you can see there are two possible extremes for anyone made redundant. At one extreme someone with long service, a good redundancy package and possibly able to draw pension straight away - or have another job already lined up - may think they have won the lottery.

At the other extreme, redundancy with little or no payout can mean homes being lost, serious issues for children and in some cases it can affect the mental health of the person who loses the position of breadwinner.

When I look back at my career I have been at both extremes. When I bought my first house with a mortgage that seemed impossibly large (£20,000, I seem to remember) redundancy would have been a real worry. When I made the decision to leave my employer to set up my own business, redundancy would have been my former employers 'sponsoring' my new venture and giving me a clear year to set things up - alas there was none on offer.

So how do you maintain respect? There are a number of pointers:

■ Be as open and honest as possible. Keep people in the loop and make sure they don't hear things from others that they should have heard from you.

■ Genuinely try to help people get interviews with either alternate departments in your company or use any networks you have built up externally to help with outside companies.

■ If at all possible try to avoid sensitive periods. If it can wait until mid January why spoil Christmas by doing it just before?

■ Don't do the really crass thing of being seen to spend money on 'luxuries' when taking peoples' livelihood away. Probably

a bad day to have the new company 'top of the range' Merc
delivered

■ Remember David Brent in *'The Office'* saying that there was
some bad news and some good news? The bad news was a lot
of redundancies but the good news was that he himself had got
promotion! I know this is a comedy sketch but you wouldn't
need to go far to find a similar real example. Take extra care
not to openly communicate good messages to some in front of
those who are being disappointed. Be subtle.

■ If seemingly 'gratuitous' money is being spent at the same
time as redundancies explain why. One company I work with
has had to make redundancies and some are wondering why the
company is spending considerable sums on an awards weekend
'jolly' for their top external distributors. It is these distributors
who are keeping the company going and maintaining work for
the remaining workforce. It is a competitive industry and they
have to do all they can to maintain the relationship with their
external 'sales force'.

■ Use measurable and justifiable reasons for one person being
displaced instead of another. Remember the job is redundant,
not the person. Use proper open processes to assess who is most
suitable for the jobs that remain. See the section on 'Favourites'.

TIP Openness and honesty along with a realisation of the effect, good or bad, that the decision is having will benefit both
you and your team. Respect can increase and the productivity
of those not being made redundant in the team will be better
in a very difficult period.

UNDERSTANDING

This section looks at your understanding of your team. How they operate and how you can gain the most respect and therefore get the most from them.

Favouritism

I never have favourites. Ummm. Human nature programmes us to like some things more than others. Just think how bland life would be if cabbage tasted as good as chocolate, if sprouts tasted like sweets to kids.

The same applies to people- we can't help but like some more than others. If we liked everyone the same, meeting a partner would be easy - just hold a lucky dip. Wars would be harder to start (even for certain world leaders…). You will, as a boss, as a human being (this probably excludes one or two I have worked for) like some of your team more than others. Fact.

Therefore it is essential that you are conscious of that before looking at yourself and where you might show unfounded favouritism. Favouritism is not giving someone a better rise because they are good, it is not about promoting someone on merit. **Favouritism is:**

■ Sharing business secrets with the ones you like to the exclusion of others with no good business reason

■ Openly being friendlier with some than others in the office environment. My wife worked for one manager who used to walk in past most of his team without saying a word, sit with his back to them and then phone his 'favourite' to come and have a chat - every morning (he sat 5 desks away)! This favourite was not senior to any other members but was, as the team put it, 'One of the Tufty club'. The manager here showed a complete lack of respect to the majority of the team and the individual who they 'befriended', who through no fault of their own lost respect in the team.

■ Allowing unfair privileges to favourites (going home early, starting late, parking spaces etc.)

■ Blatant preferential promotions training courses and the like.

■ Going to lunch or a drink straight after work always with favourites to the exclusion of others

The list can go and on but you can see that the manager must be acutely aware of the potential for favouritism to be read into every act.

Relatives

How about where husbands and wives work for each other in a large company? Please, please, please don't do it – unless it is a genuine family business. It is unfair on the boss, the spouse and the rest of the team. Even if the spouse is brilliant at his/her job the team will say it was because of the relationship that promotions, rises etc were given. If the spouse is useless – how does the manager deal with it 'You're fired! And by the way, who is picking up the kids and what's for dinner tonight?'

Most large companies have rules against this BUT they are often broken. Another large company I was involved with had a sales director who married his secretary. They carried on working together which meant they couldn't enforce the rules at a local branch where a woman working for her husband was causing issues. 'But it's all right for you…'

That relationship in the local branch was a TOTAL disaster. A disaster for the reasons mentioned above and lots of others. If anyone muttered anything derogatory about the boss in the branch (and surprise, surprise this does happen, even to the best bosses) the individual was instantly summoned to the bosses office for a dressing down. His partner fed everything back better than a bush telegraph. Not a happy place and no respect evident for the boss or his partner.

The theme that applies here is consistency. Your behaviour must be consistent in terms of how you deal with staff. Think. What innocent acts are giving the impression of favouritism? Have you been for a drink after work with the same group to the exclusion of others too often? Do you openly invite certain people for lunch without specific reason or without inviting others too often?

TIP Be aware. If you aren't aware of how you can appear to have favourites - you can't possibly deal with it. Like many things you can't deal with an issue until you realise you have one. Confess 'My name is: XXXXX: I am a manager - I have favourites...'

What drives people (don't assume they are all like you)

One of the things that makes us respect someone is that they are (genuinely) interested in us. I quote Richard Denny, a speaker and author I respect and have spoken to many times who says, 'To be **interesting** you have to be **interested**'. You can also substitute 'interesting for 'respected'. The boss who understands what drives his or her people and uses it will gain respect.

What drives you as a boss? Salary, bonus, better car, status, power? Probably one or all of these, whether you admit it or not. I have no wish to get technical and go into theories and business models because they are often boring and meaningless in the work environment. However I will go into one small bit of theory. Maslow's hierarchy of needs spells out what drives us. It is very simple to see that someone working for you, earning less money, may well be driven by the basic needs, physiological (shelter, food, water) or safety of their family. Potentially you have left those needs behind and are driven by the social, esteem and self actualisation needs. What does that mean in English?

```
        SELF ACTUALISATION
         ESTEEM NEEDS
         SOCIAL NEEDS
         SAFETY NEEDS
      PHYSIOLOGICAL NEEDS
```

What this means is that the effort you put into your work (which may be misguided) and is reflected in long hours, no breaks, weekend working and the like, does not reflect how your team needs to balance their lives. Take a person who is responsible for a young or elderly dependant. What are their needs? Probably the security of the money to cope along with the need to fit the job in around the care duties. Potentially a lot different to yours.

How does this relate to respect? Do you think it gains respect when you keep someone late in a meeting when you know that they have an outside responsibility that meets entirely with their contracted hours? Do you think it gains respect when you don't even acknowledge the issue when asking for more? (It didn't work for Oliver). Does it gain respect when you ask for jobs to be done that you know cannot be done in the time allotted?

This is not saying don't ask for more, it is not saying you can't ask someone to work later, it is not saying you can't ask someone to go away for a few days on work. It is saying that you HAVE to acknowledge what you are asking and help the individual make the arrangements to do it. Give them notice - allow time off in lieu. Think about HOW you can achieve what you want while respecting their needs, which, as stated, may be very different to yours.

Make sure you manage others time as well as your own. Do you even see the person who is so desperate for the job they will do anything to keep it? Look at the sweat shops in far flung places making cheap clothes for example. They are so desperate for work that they do ridiculous hours, take ridiculous risks. Because their needs are right at the bottom of the hierarchy. The words exploitation and abuse come to mind. You have a responsibility you need to take seriously to gain respect.

TIP If you understand what makes people tick use it to your mutual advantage. Someone who has to care for a young or elderly relative might prefer time off to being paid overtime for the extra hours they have worked. You might not have a process but a little common sense goes a long way to gaining respect.

Staff rewards

Some companies show an enlightened approach when it comes to giving managers budgets to reward staff. A voucher here, a meal there, perhaps an adventure day or the like. Unbelievably a percentage of managers don't use their allowance! The time limit expires, they pass the money to someone else or just generally forget they have it.

If they deliberately don't use it the reasons are, "We are busy – they can't take the time off", "The rewards are small and don't mean much", "I forgot", "Can't be bothered with the paperwork" etc.

How de-motivating is that to the team that they know you have money to spend on them but can't be bothered? Unless all of your team are completely undeserving of any award at all (in which case question your own recruitment, training and motivation skills) please don't fail to spend money. Small awards that might not turn you on may mean a lot to the team.

TIP Use it or lose them! If you have a chance of rewarding good loyal staff - use it. Never assume that what seems 'small beer' to you doesn't mean a lot to the team.

Know the family

What? This is work not a social club! Test yourself. Do you know the names of your employees wives/husbands, their children and the children's ages? What do their wives/husbands do for a living? Are there any difficult home circumstances, elderly relatives that need looking after for example? If you don't know, why don't you?

You need to understand what makes people tick to gain their respect. If they have children you can have legal obligations in regard to flexible working and the like, but why do we need the law to deal with these things? Because people show a complete lack of respect or understanding of the issues surrounding any type of care responsibility, or other external commitments.

We wouldn't have laws against murder and violence if everybody had always cared, shown respect and not hurt each other for the last zillion years. Ridiculous? - it's not! Whether you believe Adam and Eve or Darwin's theory of evolution no-one thought 'what happens if someone murders or deliberately harms someone else?' - until it happened.

Employment law is no different. If employers weren't guilty of some pretty awful practices over the years there wouldn't need to be any working hours, race, sex or age discrimination laws. Most of the 'really annoying' HR type laws are there because people abuse other people and show a complete lack of respect. Think! So we now know why rules and laws are necessary. Please don't be the next reason why another law is passed...

Make time to know your people. How are their children after chicken pox, flu or any other lurgy that has caused your employee stress. Respect the fact that he/she might need to leave early or work from home for a period while the child is ill.

You need to give these matters the emphasis they deserve. You getting your priorities right with your team WILL reward you in greater output and favours from them when the chips are down and you need some help. Perhaps when there is no overtime available. Build the bank of good will!

TIP Test yourself. Challenge yourself to talk to two team members a day about their home life. Use their partners or children's names, 'How is Ben doing with his SATs test?', 'Is Dan's job ok with the cut back announcements at his firm?'. Boy, you will sound as if you care. Respect!

Socialising

A perennial issue. How do you deal with socialising with the team while maintaining or even gaining respect? Again honesty is a good policy. Some people, believe it or not, get very silly, irresponsible, downright objectionable or lecherous when under the influence of a few drinks (some on VERY few drinks and some achieve a full house!).

What would your friends tell you? What does your wife/husband tell you? Would they say yes this applies to you? If so, the simple rule about drinking with your team is… DON'T.

How can you maintain respect when (if you are a man) the girls have had to peel you off at frequent intervals, you claim that you are staring at their chest to see if they have name badges on, you profess undying love and that your wife/girlfriend doesn't understand you. Or, is it you dancing in the village pond with your underpants on your head or challenging the local 'boys' to 'come outside'? These things happen.

I guarantee that if you get a group of 10 employees together who have been at work for at least 5 years and ask them about bosses who have done some very silly things when they are drunk – they would be able to write a book, not just a chapter.

Even if you behave impeccably when you have had 15 pints and 2 bottles of wine it is still not a good idea. The thing that loosens quicker than clothing with alcohol intake is tongues. Alcohol does reduce inhibitions in all sorts of ways and you WILL say something to a minimum of one person that you shouldn't – guaranteed. Therefore the rules apply to you as well.

So how do you walk the tightrope between this and being a bore who doesn't socialise with the team. **There are rules:**

■ Don't attend ALL the informal events – sometimes the team will want a night out without you (hard to understand that one isn't it?)

■ When you go to an event use the drink driving laws as a good guide to your own alcohol consumption. Always take the car and that will stop you drinking.

■ You should be there at most team events and put your hand in your pocket. When there is £20 going into the kitty put your £20 in even if you are only going to have 2 apple juices. Nothing looks worse than the boss who says 'I won't put into the kitty as I am only staying for a couple - I will buy my own'. That breaches several human behaviour rules and probably a few European Directives as well! One or two of my old managers please note.

■ When the event really gets going and you can see that everyone is getting 'well oiled' do what the News of the World reporters allegedly do ('The gorgeous blond approached me wearing nothing more than a smile with an offer I could only dream of - so I made my excuses and left...'). You have made your appearance now make your excuse.

■ Try to encourage activities that do not lead themselves to excessive behaviour. It will happen. A senior Police Officer told me recently that one change he has noticed is that there are often very drunk off duty Police Officers at clubs and bars when they get called there. No matter how much we would like our teams to behave responsibly at all times it won't always happen - just don't be around when it gets this far.

Yes you should devote time to team activities. Use the resources at hand to help get the most from your teams and make them gell. Plan the events you will go to which MUST be all the formal ones and some of the informal. Be selective over the informal events although being a boring **** is no excuse for not going to the restaurant where 'the music is too loud', 'I don't like Uzbekistan food', 'My husband/wife has a crochet evening and I can't get babysitters'.

TIP Attend all formal team events within the guidelines above. With the ad-hoc socials attend enough to avoid any accusations of aloofness and put your hand in your pocket!

Respect and utilise skills - don't be frightened!

I'm the boss, so I know best about everything there is to know. Yeah right. To gain the respect of your team understand what their skills are. The 99% likelihood is that there are people in the team who do parts of your job better than you (150% likelihood for some I could mention). Your job is to recognise and harness that.

Example: you have to arrange a conference to reward your top achievers. You have no experience in this at all but you have someone in the team who used to work for a conference management company - use them. Brief them on the overall plan and objective and let them come up with the ideas and the project plan. This type of thing is best seen and illustrated on some of the team building events we have all been on. No matter what the task the manager takes the lead.

I ran a team building event a while ago where one of the tasks was to get teams to complete an assault course task (you know the sort of thing - make a boat and get 15 people to a desert island using a piece of string, a wine bottle and a tooth brush). One of the more junior members of the team was in the TA and much more suited to the task than the 'boss'. Did he lead the task? - No! The boss was in charge come what may. Unsurprisingly he made a hash of it ('If only I had two toothbrushes and the string had been longer…') - the TA guy would have won the task for them. Yes, you could argue that he should have spoken up. But had the boss created an atmosphere where this was not encouraged? Speak when you are spoken to! Don't challenge me - I am the boss.

We are straying into business culture here but: do you respect someone who will listen? Do you respect someone who will acknowledge others' ideas? Do you respect someone who succeeds by taking the team with them? Yes, yes and yes. Being a consultative boss is one of the most motivating factors there is for staff (research for the Institute of Leadership and Management).

Remember – prioritise to peoples strengths – including yours. A good manager doesn't always 'do' but they know how to get a job done.

TIP Do you know what skills your team have? I bet a lot of you think that you do - you may even have done the personality assassination tests - you know the ones that let you see whether people are completer finishers, movers and shapers or just paperweights. Where everyone answers the questions and are then surprised about what the test tells them! 'Goodness me, I ticked a box that said I hate completing jobs and it says I am not a completer finisher - wow! How did it do that?!'

As an example I once struggled in an early interview to give an example of decision making. The job I was in, like many, corporate jobs, meant decisions were only taken by bosses via feasibility groups, steering committees and working groups - and that was just to establish who went for lunch at what time.

Using the criteria based approach I could not demonstrate my decision making ability. The manager gave me a very full debrief after the (unsuccessful) interview and in terms of job interviews that was the best coaching I have ever had. She gave me a number of tips but the main one came from her on discovering that I was a Special Constable outside work. I was making decisions about people's liberty - not how many paper clips they could have. She told me that if I had mentioned that at the interview I would probably have got the job.

BUSINESS CULTURE

In this section we will look at things that tend to be categorised as 'Business Culture' issues. Some will be cultures 'from above' and some that you create.

Dress code

How does dress impact on respect? Let me give you a real example. A High Street Bank has a Head Office in London. They have decided that smart casual clothing is the order of the day unless in customer facing situations. Not an unusual position these days. This goes from the chief executive to the most junior member of staff.

One department has a head who has decided to buck this trend and wants his team to have 'standards'. He wants not only collar and tie but shirts MUST be white (didn't that go out in Victorian times? 'Albert - not without a white shirt, you naughty boy!'). **How does this make his team feel?**

■ It is great that they have standards different to everyone else,

■ They are delighted to be the only team of c-30 that have to wear ties in an office that houses 8,000 people,

■ They enjoy having the 'mickey' taken out of them in the canteen?

No - they think he is out of order and has his priorities wrong. If he personally wants to wear a tie, or a bow tie or a flashing tie that spins when he is angry that's fine - but he shouldn't impose his own unique style on those around him.

How ridiculous to lose respect over something so trivial and something that won't get an ounce of extra work out of his team. In fact the impact of the loss of respect if added to other issues will actually reduce output. Don't forget the effect on your bosses' respect for you as well as the team's respect for you. What are you saying to your boss if you don't go along with his or her policy? You are better than them? You know better than them? You can lose respect from above as well as below.

Another real example involved another company where there was a dress down policy every Friday. Again, one area decided that 'they had standards' and the boss annoyed everyone by insisting that they stayed in full business dress. He told everyone around the rest of the business that it was his team who insisted on staying that way as THEY wanted to look business-like and didn't agree with the new policy - it wasn't.

One day they invited the MD to a meeting on a Friday. All suited and booted they awaited the arrival of the MD who came in, in a pair of chinos and an open necked shirt. His first question was, 'Why don't you all join with the rest of us and dress down on Fridays - you stick out, you appear aloof'. Lots of stares at the boss showed the MD that it wasn't the team - it was the boss for his own self agenda (whatever that was - perhaps he liked to wear a tie to bed or perhaps his wife still dressed him in the morning.) The red face of the boss was also a bit of a giveaway.

That was the last Friday on which they didn't dress down. Not only had the boss lost some respect but the whole team had had to put up with being made fun of by colleagues from around the business. What happened next? Because the team had been 'repressed' from the company policy they pushed all the rules and started wearing jeans and other clothing that was barred - the boss then had to waste loads more time dealing with that. (As a matter of fact they introduced a no boobs, bums or tums policy much to the horror of several directors!) Every action has an equal and opposite reaction...

How much time was wasted on this non productive issue? Look at where you spend your time. Prioritise what is important and what is not. Will wearing a tie make me more efficient when perhaps I don't want to be forced to wear one? Will I be less efficient in a blue or a pink shirt than a white one? This is not specifically about dress standards but the principle of why waste time fighting the tide when there is no benefit to you or your team (apart, possibly, from your own ego).

Be consistent – the team will know that if there is a general rule that they can wear pink spotted luminous leather shorts then they should expect to be treated consistently with peers where there is no justifiable business reason not to. (If you pay me I will tell you where this particular rule applies.)

The principle here is don't buck what is stated company policy especially when it is to no advantage to your team. The only excuse for ever bucking company policy is if you are doing it **for** your team.

TIP Don't lose respect over a non-issue.

Catch someone doing something well today

A really valuable business principle that is ignored most of the time. Except, that is for the normal one week after coming back from a training course covering this area...

Do you respect someone who only ever speaks to you when there is something wrong? 'Oh no here comes the boss, what have I done wrong?' I once had to present to a group of Senior Managers in London when I worked for a major High Street Bank. The audience included one of the Group General

Managers – in business terms one step below (below?) God. I thought the session went OK.

Next morning when I got in to work the Sales Director (who could be very scary) was waiting by my desk. My heart sank…

'Martin' he said, 'XXXX the General Manager phoned me late last night' gulp, 'to say well done – a great job. Keep it up!' Fantastic, he had made a special effort to say well done and had caught me doing something good. This boss was totally consistent – mess up and you knew about it – do well and you also knew about it.

How often do you (yes I know you are busy, deadlines, hassle from above, etc.etc.etc.) catch someone doing something well?

The respect you will gain is immense. If it doesn't come naturally (sadly a very high percentage of managers are not there due to their natural people skills) make a diary note or put it on your 'to do' list. This is serious! If you want lasting impact this has to become part of the norm – not a two week fad while the course/book/self study is fresh in mind.

Companies spend thousands on 'reward' processes. Unfortunately many have missed the point that saying thank you for a job well done is not a process. Just imagine one of your team completes a good piece of work within time under budget and the big bosses are very happy. You start the thank you process (in the privacy of your own office), fill in the required forms, get them countersigned by HR (after a two week wait while the HR partner is on holiday), and pass them up the line for senior manager sign off. Then after your holiday you are able to present the member of staff with £250 holiday vouchers (6 weeks after the event). Great!

In an ideal world how should this work? Dependent on the level of work undertaken the member of staff should have been thanked personally by the boss as soon as possible – and probably by the boss's boss as well. So far this has cost the company nothing but the member of staff feels good. Don't faint, but maybe you could take the employee to lunch or buy them a bottle of champagne – out of your own pocket if necessary – if you can't claim it back think about the impact on your career, bonus etc. If it is appropriate to go down the reward 'process' fine but make sure the employee knows what you are doing and how long it will take – and say thank you in the meantime.

Which approach has the biggest effect on morale and creates respect for the boss – the instant thank you or nothing for 6 weeks and then £250 vouchers? You might be surprised. Actually the combination of both is the best one BUT we must realise that a process NEVER replaces simple courtesies.

TIP Think - when did you last catch someone doing something well? If you aren't good at this naturally put a diary note in! If you only have a handful of direct reports ask them who has done something well today. Don't forget it could be one of them… Take the time to say thanks - it only takes a few seconds.

Blame culture

One of the very best ways you can successfully achieve a complete loss of respect is by implementing a vibrant blame culture. You can think of mottos such as 'The blame lies anywhere but here', 'It wasn't me I didn't do it', 'Let's find someone to blame' or perhaps 'Sacrificial lambs rule ok'.

A recent survey for the Institute of Leadership and Management stated that the thing most people dislike most about a manager is one who always looks for someone to blame. This factor was ranked almost twice as high as the next one (expecting staff to do as they are told with no debate).

Let's be clear, this is not identifying who has made an error, who needs more training, who needs a warning or the like. It is the unedifying culture of desperately trying to pin something on someone to 'save your own backside'. In some organisations cowardice increases with rank. The higher you are the more frightened you are of where the buck stops - it stops anywhere but here.

Look at the 'Walk the Talk' section for a good example.

If you have a reputation for being a blame manager you will NOT have the respect of your team. Almost twice as many of your team will be looking to leave as those in teams where this culture does not exist. You will actually put people off wanting to be managers at all (information from the website of the Institute of Leadership and Management) as twice as many people who have had this bad experience don't want to progress to that particular role. How important is that? You can actually put people off being managers themselves!

Very few major errors in business are the result of one thing or one person (usually decisions are hidden behind so many committees and project groups that you can't find out who did what any way). Usually a combination of factors, people and/or systems are at fault. Good management finds out what went wrong and puts it right.

If it was an innocent error or a lack of training, deal with it. If the same person continues to make the same mistake, deal with it.

But don't spend your whole time looking for people to blame. You know what? If too many mistakes happen in your team through processes or people, look in the mirror – you may see where the real blame lies (in a no blame culture sort of way).

Don't waste time witch hunting. Blame culture spreads like wildfire. If the team is used to being blamed it will develop strategies learnt from you – to blame someone else. You will have less and less chance of quickly finding out where fault lies and dealing with it.

One of my team was very used to being blamed, often publicly, by her previous manager. The first time I was in a meeting with her another senior manager started to blame her over something our team had done. I stopped him and said – no, if there was fault it is mine as the manager of the area – I would deal with it. Effect? He was shocked. He had never heard someone take the blame as a manager and she was shocked as I hadn't blamed her in public, or stood by while someone else blamed her. We got on very well after that and she blossomed by not being a 'whipping boy' for everything that went wrong. She eventually became my trusted number 2 and with increasing confidence came a lot more output. (In fact the error HAD BEEN her fault but only due to the complete lack of guidance and training for the job in hand). The other senior manager never tried the open 'blame culture' approach with her again.

Make sure the team knows where you are coming from. If you are trying to find out what happened they know why and will help establish the situation. They also know that anyone who is consistently incompetent will get the right help and then the P45 if nothing else can be done. The rest of the team will RE-SPECT you for dealing with a long term problem – even if the problem is a colleague – as long as you do it right.

TIP If it is your area of responsibility take it on the chin. Then manage the way to stop it ever happening again.

Complaints culture

This area is very closely linked to Blame Culture. 'Oh no, we have had a complaint – I had better try to keep it quiet so the boss doesn't blame me.' This attitude is very unhealthy for the individual, the complainant and the business. You will find huge respect for the boss who encourages a culture of being open and honest with complaints.

Complaints are a life blood of a business. You can do all the market research you want but when it gets to the 'sharp end', complaints tell you what is going wrong, what customers don't like and what you need to put right. Some companies, where there are laws surrounding complaints, such as financial services have procedures in place and timescales for dealing with everything.

But, what is essential, is that lessons are learned. Complaints mainly stem from two areas, a system problem or an individual's error. Where it is a system problem make sure it gets dealt with or at least ensure there is a work around in place to stop the event happening again while the issue is sorted out.

If it is an individual's error make sure that the training and guidance is in place to deal with it. Communicate effectively – make sure the individual understands what they did wrong, ask 'What would you do next time you have this situation?'

For every complainant that tells you they have an issue there could be another 10 who don't bother and just move their business elsewhere. Dealing with the cause of that complaint could save your business thousands or more. If the culture is one where the complaint gets 'hidden' you are losing money from day one.

Research at the multinational bank I worked for showed that the most loyal customers and those most likely to purchase further were those where a mistake had been made BUT it had been put right in an exemplary manner. My 'bright idea' submitted to the bank's award programme that we deliberately make a mistake on all new accounts, and put it right, wasn't even acknowledged – can't think why.

This does go to prove however that getting something wrong is not necessarily the end of the world – it is how you deal with the problem that creates respect from the team and loyalty from the customers.

TIP If people are frightened of admitting to complaints you need to look at the culture you are creating

Trust!

Do you trust your team? Do you let them make decisions? One of the most demoralising things for staff and therefore a serious dent in the respect they have for you is the lack of trust you show when it comes to their making decisions.

How can you respect someone who always has to take control, always has the last word and ends up working 23 hours a day because they won't let go of anything? I have heard people say that a manager who reports to them is a real hard worker, he/she works all hours and weekends to get the job done. Maybe they are just stupid. Maybe they can't delegate, maybe they don't trust trustworthy staff. They may look like a hard worker but in truth they lose all respect of a team that starts to work at half pace 'because it's not worth it'. They work, and look, absolutely shattered all the time and make mistakes.

I remember once reporting to a boss who reported directly to the CEO of a major worldwide organisation. He was so scared of making a decision and not trusted by the CEO that even very low level decisions went to the top. In frustration one day

I told my boss that I was going to call the CEO direct. His face was a picture! 'Why?' He stuttered. 'Oh' I said, 'I want to know if I can go for lunch ½ hour earlier than usual.' He didn't get it (he had been in Australia for years and didn't understand good old British sarcasm). The point was the complete lack of trust shown caused huge problems in the team. The CEO didn't trust his report, therefore the report didn't trust anyone under him to make a decision and so it went on down the line.

If the team is not up to the task – look in the mirror.

A team that is given responsibility and the authority to deal with issues makes for a more motivated team. The boss who encourages this gains respect. The boss who makes sure his team is able to carry out the job efficiently rather than do it themself gains respect. When people are new to you, work with them – make joint decisions until you are happy that they know their role. If that doesn't happen have you recruited correctly? Have you trained correctly?

Another example: I worked for one boss who had a tough reputation. For the first 6 months I was proving my worth. I came across a situation where I had to make a decision to withdraw a senior manager's authority to undertake a role he was in due to a long history of incompetence. My boss, who should have been making the decision, was away on holiday. I knew that he hated being presented with problems and would rather be presented with solutions. I did the deed and the cat was amongst the pigeons.

On his return from holiday I saw my boss straight away and told him what I had done, why I had done it, why I hadn't waited for him to return and the previous steps that had been taken to deal with the situation.

His response? 'Well done – don't worry about any 'flack' I will deal with that.' He did. Decision ratified. How did I feel? I felt that my boss trusted me and as long as I did a good job with the correct evidence I would be backed. Motivated, confident.

Here is an example of a less than satisfactory approach. A team member had a huge amount of experience in putting together award events. This included dealing with top London restaurants and celebrity chefs amongst other high profile venues. The team member had been thanked for her work on previous occasions for arranging events very well (so far so good). Out of the blue and for no reason at all the next time she put together a plan for an event the top manager got involved and said that he wanted to get someone more senior to check the venue first.

That more senior manager had no experience, would not have known what to look for in a venue if it hit him in the face and added absolutely nothing to the process. The boss already had a full report, photos, reviews from high profile magazines and full costings. How did this make the team member concerned feel? Undervalued, not trusted, wondering what was wrong with the previous events.

All because she didn't have the right 'grade' after her name in the bureaucratic hierarchy. The boss would rather have a senior manager, incompetent at that particular process, look at the venue than a really proven team member. What did it cost the company? Hundreds of pounds or more, with extra time wasted and the risk that they lost a popular venue because of the extra time delays. What did it cost the boss? Respect. Stories like this circulate like wildfire.

What could he have done? He could have asked the team member to take said manager and show them the ropes, show them what to look for and how to go about negotiations. The boss then gets respect from team member who is trusted enough to train the manager and gets respect from the manager who realises that he/she won't be left with a project they know little about. One way zero respect, one way respect x2.

Research in late 2007 (for Investors in People) showed that less than $1/3$ of employees had trust in their manager with 8 out of 10 believing their manager had let them down in some way. Surprisingly the longer someone works for a boss the less they trust them! A bit sad but the trust in the boss is highest amongst those that hardly know them. To gain trust you have to give trust. Read between the lines. Gaining trust = gaining respect.

How much time do you waste by not trusting people? Of course when you have a new team member you need to establish their competencies. But when you have done that make sure you use their abilities to the full.

TIP Trust in your team is a greater motivator than pay. If you don't give trust you lose respect. If you don't gain trust you lose respect. Lose respect and you lose good workers.

TIP When people are new to you work with them - make joint decisions until you are happy that they know their role. If that doesn't happen have you recruited correctly? Have you trained correctly?

ACTIONS

Here are some simple things that you can do to start increasing the respect you get from the team.

Expenses

Why on earth is the subject of expenses in this book? Just think about it. Your team may, or may not, be in the same financial position as you. If you are tight for money you will understand the need to get money owed to you paid quickly. If you aren't – think about the impact on your employees if their money is not quickly forthcoming.

What happens if that trip away for two days and 400 miles in petrol is not reimbursed quickly. Does that mean that the employee can't pay off the credit card, incurring interest charges? Does it mean a bounced cheque at the bank? It may mean none of these but if you delay paying rightfully claimed expenses YOU could be causing a great deal of stress. Dealing with employee matters that affect their lives is a priority! Make sure you understand that. If you are going to be absent make sure you have advised everyone of the process while you are away. Absence is no excuse. There should be a recognised 'plan B' even if your absence is unexpected (someone has to win the lottery).

TIP Assume that everyone needs the money they claim for as a matter of urgency. It is not for you to judge whether people need expenses paid quickly or not.

Be seen

Heard the phrase children should be seen and not heard? Well bosses should be seen and heard. How can you hope to gain respect if you are remote? Do you have an office? Is the door always closed? Could you sit in the general office instead? No rules here, but just think about what you want to achieve and how best to do it. Will moving into the general office inhibit your team? I would suggest that if you haven't got the respect and relationships right then it probably will.

Most offices these days are open plan with only the very, very big bosses shut away, so you probably don't have to face that issue. However you would be amazed at the lengths some bosses go to, so they can avoid the hideous process of having to talk to their team, to swap small talk, to have to think of things to say that are not work related. Email to the rescue for them. Sad but true.

How do you improve your visibility? Get outside your comfort zone! Good managers know what has to be done and then work out strategies to do it. If some parts of 'Being Seen' are outside your normal scope of activities – get help. There are more courses and self help guides (and books like this – ed) than most people have had hot dinners. Use them. Most managers have a shelf or cupboard full of course notes, self help guides and the like completely untouched by human hand.

How is this related to respect? – By improving your communication skills and visibility you can gain the respect of your team.

Example: An old MD of mine was awful as a public speaker or in a social situation with staff. Shy, not confident, stuttering and with no 'presence' at all. The company recognised his undoubted talents (he was the most respected MD I have ever worked for or been involved with - see

Walk the Talk) and spent money providing him with relevant coaching. Over the course of two years he became not just competent but polished in the art of public speaking. He became more than just comfortable in a social situation, which allowed him to work closer with his team. It wasn't the training that got him there it was his attitude to the training. He worked hard, got outside his comfort zone and took feedback - what he didn't do was put the training guide in his bottom drawer. Everyone knew the amount of effort he put in and that gained him the utmost respect.

If you can't talk to people you can't actually put into practice much of what has been written previously. Time is always the issue. It takes time away from your emails, your desk, your work to be visible. Make time - it will increase your respect and your team's output.

TIP Make time in your diary. Make sure no-one puts you in back to back meetings all day. You can't be seen if you are always in closed meetings.

Public Speaking

Some people love it - some people hate it but all managers have to do it. Being heard in public can do wonders for a) gaining respect or b) losing respect. Your choice.

First let's get out of the ostrich position - head in sand ignoring everything going on around you - it will happen if you want to 'make the grade' at any level. You can't avoid it. Having established that, what can you do to make sure you achieve a) above rather than b) above?

First and most importantly beware the manager who says - 'I don't need to rehearse - I am better just 'winging' it'. Probably 1 in 1,000 managers can get away with this approach. For us mere mortals that way of going about things is doomed to failure. What will happen? You will run over time, you will meander, you will get lost, you will use slides as your prompt (rather than visuals illustrating your point), you will hide behind the lectern where your notes are, you will confuse the audience, you might let bad language 'slip' that you wouldn't do ideally, you might make flippant remarks that can be seen as sexist, racist, ageist or in fact any other 'ist' or 'ism'.

I went to a roadshow run by the CEO of a major international organisation. Three hours of strategy, long term goals and short term aims. It had a lot of impressive aspects. However the CEO kept making derogatory remarks about his wife, in a light hearted way. 'I need to get the share price up as my wife keeps spending it' 'I don't need to do market research I just look at her credit card statement.'

His audience were 70% women and after the event a high percentage of the conversation was about his demeaning remarks regarding his wife - which were seen to apply to women in general - not about the great strategy and vision. What a waste.

In terms of bad language I have only ever seen a 'serious' swear word used once in a business scenario to good effect. That was by a professional compere who was practiced and knew his audience. I have seen 'serious' swear words used several other times and that is all people talk about afterwards - losing the benefit of the rest of the session. I am not going to repeat how the compere made it work so you are not tempted!

Are you known as a good public speaker or are you in the majority who need help? There is no shame in needing help, there is shame in ploughing on knowing you need it but not asking for it. Look again at the example in the previous section (Be seen). An impressive show in public will boost the respect you get from your team and your 'lords and masters' - what an opportunity.

TIPS Use the various coaching aids available. Our guide is to use the 12 Ps (further information available from the author and Denny Publishing).

Presentation – how you appear, tie, no tie, casual, formal?

Position – please don't hide behind the lectern.

Prompts – use cue cards – we are not all great thespians.

Positioning – use the News at 10 approach – tell them what you are going to tell them, tell them and then tell them what you have told them – three for the price of one!

Practice – there is no excuse for a lack of practice or rehearsal. Rehearse until it looks natural.

Passion – think about how your body language is when you are passionate about a subject – I know it is hard to enthuse about last month's sales of widgets but try.

Pace, Power, Pause – these are the most powerful ways to engage your audience. They need practice and they need someone who knows what they are doing to show you how. Do you know you can reduce all ambient noise in the room to zero by controlling the power of your voice? Sometimes the punch line is best delivered quietly – let them strain to listen actively rather than beating their eardrums with your sheer volume.

Please don't (it's a P ok?) swear or any 'ism' – it's not worth it.

PowerPoint – PowerPoint is the most overused presentation medium there is. It is overused as a script on the screen. Who has heard the phrase 'Those of you at the back won't be able to see the small print' – so why is it there? Doesn't the back half of the audience matter as much? Keep information on screen to a minimum and make sure the slide follows you – not the other way round. PowerPoint is not a script for a lazy presenter.

PowerPoint – PowerPoint is also the most underused presentation medium there is. Use in expert hands can really enhance a presentation. But please don't try all the new slide changes you have discovered in one presentation – the audience gets dizzy!

Appraisals

Don't we all love appraisals? How can you use an appraisal to gain respect? In fact there are several ways.

Honesty

Lack of surprises

Not a tick box exercise

OK one by one. **Honesty** – we are all honest aren't we? An example: I employed a really good guy in one particular role. He was highly trained, motivated and over time could bring a lot to this new role for which he was learning the ropes. His one down side was that in terms of performance rating (which drove pay and bonus) he always thought he should be a 1+ (on a scale of 1 to 5 where 1 was achieved by only approximately 1% of people, 3 was the norm and 5 was better start looking for another job pdq).

As usual in a big company bell curves applied. If you were a fantastic manager who developed a great team they were punished by the 'You have to have 1 x 1, 2 x 2 15 x 3 and a sacrifice.' approach employed – even to small teams. (Don't start me I could write another book on that one).

Back to this guy. He had been with me for 8 months of the year when it came to annual appraisal. I genuinely thought he rated a 3 – by far the most popular grade and one which reflected a job well done. He wasn't happy. We had had a lot of discussion during the year and all of the good points and development points had been well discussed and documented so there were no surprises there.

He said after a thorough discussion, 'I guess you are under pressure regarding grades and you need to make sure you have enough 3's so that's what I am – the same happened last year when my manager explained how it was.' 'No.' I said. 'A 3 is what you are.' Silence.

He came round quite quickly after oxygen and CPR. After a bit more discussion he said, and I quote word for word, 'I don't agree with you but I RESPECT you for being HONEST and not hiding behind someone else.'

So there it is – honesty was a novelty to him. What happened next – he did brilliantly as he developed into the role, got promoted and now holds a senior role. I have no doubt he is excellent and always thinks he is a 1+!

Is this really novel?

Late in 2007 YouGov conducted some research for Investors in People. Scarily:

44% of employees don't think their boss is always honest with them in appraisals.

29% think appraisals are a waste of time as a result.

21% actually think their appraisal was unfair.

23% think their managers see appraisals as a tick-box exercise.

19% say the manager hasn't even thought about the appraisal until they are in the room.

Only 21% of managers follow up on what is discussed.

These facts speak for themselves. How can any self respecting manager earn respect while completing appraisals in such a disorganised and dishonest way?

No surprises – There are no excuses for any surprise at an annual review – other than a positive one! You have recommended a promotion, you have recommended a larger than usual pay rise, they are being sent on a 'prized' development course. You CANNOT suddenly hit someone with a major development issue or something they did wrong 6 months ago if you didn't mention it at the time. How could they have a chance to put it right?

Or have you saved those negative points up to justify a particular rating? Sorry but this happens all the time and is the result of either a weak system or a weak manager.

A few years ago a colleague of mine was caught going through some confidential records. He should not have been doing so. The boss said absolutely nothing for 4 weeks and then brought up the issue at his annual appraisal. My colleague had forgotten all about it – deal with these things at the time. He was wrong, he should have been reprimanded at the time and then it would have been valid to bring it up at the appraisal. If dealt with at the time the relevant 'investigation' could have happened (there could have been a valid reason – there wasn't) and the outcome dealt with. A month later at an appraisal is the wrong time to bring it up for the first time.

There are literally hundreds, no, thousands, of examples of surprises at appraisals. 'I have found that your reports are too wordy and not concise enough...' How long have you found that for? Why haven't you dealt with it? Yes this is an appraisal issue – but your appraisal not theirs! The only incompetence shown is yours as a manager.

Tick box exercise – if you think appraisals are a tick box exercise then they will be. You will let down the individual, yourself, your boss and your company. The appraisal should pull together all that has gone on during the year and be a statement of intent as to what is going to happen going forward. Remember the statistic that a pathetic 1 in 5 follow up on what is agreed in an appraisal? Be that 1 in 5 - you will gain respect as a result

Always make time to prepare effectively for an appraisal. Expect your team member to do the same. The more time you spend on preparation the more time you will save in the interview and the less likely you are to upset people and be one of the damning statistics quoted above.

Appraisals and development of your team are priorities bar none. If you do not give the prioritisation and time to this activity you deserve the negative feedback you are likely to get. You WILL lose respect here very easily in this area.

Appraisals can be a very effective method of losing respect in an instant. They can also be the way to gain long lasting respect if done correctly.

TIP Preparation, honesty and a lack of surprises should enhance your respect. Remember if you bring up any development points that were obvious for a period before the appraisal which you haven't already started to deal with, the only person who should have this marked as a negative is you.

Be aware

A slightly unusual one here. If you have ever lived in a village you will know that everyone knows everyone, who is doing what to whom and the like. It can be claustrophobic but there are major advantages. The elderly are safer as others know their movements and when to expect to see them. Children are safer as people know who belongs to whom. Teenagers who mis-behave are more likely to be spotted by someone who knows them. The news usually gets home before they do - much to their delight.

What is the point of this? You run a team, this team is your work 'village'. I am not saying that you have to be the work equivalent of the 'over the garden fence' gossip BUT you do need to keep your ear to the ground.

Amazingly not everyone will tell you everything - people will have quite serious issues that they will tell others but not you. Be aware, but don't suddenly say 'Fred tells me your wife left you for the bingo caller'. If you are aware of what is going on you can treat people more appropriately. Perhaps in this case not going to the bingo hall for the team night out.

You will pick up rumours of people getting together (work is THE best dating agency there is). It will all help you manage the team, not cause conflict - and gain respect.

Research for Investors in People (2007) showed that less than one quarter of employees would confide in their boss regarding a sensitive work related issue. Unless you have your 'ear to the ground' you can't hope to know what is going on.

No big learning points here but if you are cocooned in your own world and don't take the time to do all the other things in this book you can't hope to be aware. Teenagers would call it being street wise. Are you?

You need to make time to chat with the team. Go to lunch with some of them each week (not just the favourites - see Favouritism) - have a chat first thing or last thing.

TIP If you need formality to do this type of thing actually diary a lunch with team members once a week or make a rota. The only subject that should be banned is a direct work issue.

Firm but fair

Let no one misunderstand the fact that gaining respect does NOT equal being soft. Think about the bosses you have respected - were they soft? I doubt it. What they will have been is scrupulously fair.

If there are issues in a team - the rest of the team want you to deal with it! They do not want to work in an environment where people 'get away' with things - especially if it impacts on them. The only time you will lose the team on a matter of discipline is if you have lost their respect already.

Examples: Scenario 1. Fred is a lazy so and so. He turns up late, doesn't work very hard and is happy for the team to 'carry' him. The team respects the boss who deals with Fred. The boss does the right things in terms of warnings, coaching and so on but the situation doesn't improve. Eventually Fred gets sacked. The team say to Fred 'Sorry mate, I don't know why he did that. Still, worse things happen at sea. Good luck!'

After Fred leaves they are all relieved that they don't have to carry him anymore. The bosses' respect goes up. The team saw a firm but fair approach. The boss saw an issue and dealt with it - Fred was dragging them all down.

Scenario 2. Fred is the same lazy so and so. The boss has very little respect from the team. He also deals with the situation and moves Fred out. The team sympathise with Fred. 'How can he do that?' 'Talk about pot calling kettle…', 'It's alright for him…' 'I wouldn't trust him as far as I could throw him…'

After Fred leaves the team are deeply suspicious of the boss - respect plummets from an already low level.

What is the difference? In scenario 1 the boss works from a position of strength - i.e. the team had his respect. In scenario 2 there was no respect to start with so any difficult decision is much harder with a greater negative impact.

Another example of respect: A company I was involved with had to make a part time lady redundant as technology had effectively replaced her role. The directors hated doing it but had to make that decision for the good of the company and the other employees. What did she do on hearing the news? She wasn't happy but came in the next day with a bottle of wine for the director who had delivered the news (and no it wasn't poisoned).

Her reasons? The company was the one who had 'taken a risk' on her as someone who hadn't worked for several years due to family commitments. She was so grateful for the support she had received, the fact that they trusted her and she would get a good reference. She had so much respect for the director that she gave him a present for making her redundant! The other employees were upset but the way the situation was handled increased respect in the office.

If you don't take the time and effort to gain the respect of your team every difficult decision will be much harder than it needs to be. If you have difficult decisions to make, take the time to make sure you get them right and make sure you do them in a way that will gain the respect of the other team members wherever possible.

TIP If you have the respect of the team those difficult decisions are often nowhere as difficult as you imagine they will be. If you don't have the respect of the team they will be much harder.

Say sorry

One of the things that people respect most is someone admitting they are wrong. I guess some of you are thinking, 'but I never am'! I think back to my footballing days. The most respected referee in the league was a guy who admitted getting things wrong. On protest, if he realised he had made a mistake, he would say something like, 'Sorry lads I think I got that one wrong – I've given it now and I can't go back.' Where do you go from there? You can't berate the ref for getting it wrong – he has admitted it.

This only happened very occasionally as most times he obviously (thought he) made the right decisions. But the times he did it the respect was enormous – and people talked about it. 'He's a good bloke – at least if he realises he's got one wrong he will admit it. Not like those other jumped up...' He was no better or worse than any of the other referees technically – but had won lots more respect.

You can do the same as a manager. Admit when you get it wrong. Your team's respect for you will far outweigh the damage done by not getting it right in the first place.

A manager admitted to me recently that he went into an appraisal with a team member without doing the right preparation (he should have read the Appraisal chapter! – ed). The rating given was not reflective of the job done by the team member. After the meeting the team member asked to see him again. She said that she did not think the rating and meeting reflected her performance. He had also been feeling unhappy about the meeting, admitted to her that he was under prepared and asked to run the review meeting again. This was duly done and the new rating much more accurately reflected the true situation. Yes he should have been prepared BUT the admission and saying sorry increased his standing with this team member no end. He would never go into an appraisal meeting underprepared again either.

Walk the Talk

Why have I left this subject, which is so important, until last? That's because it is THE most important aspect of gaining respect. All of the other ideas and suggestions won't work if you don't Walk the Talk. What does that mean? It means that you act consistently, treat others equally and that you show people how to do 'it'. You lead from the front, you are a role model. Easy!

Actually it isn't. If you ask someone who has been working for 20 years how many 'role model' managers they have worked for the answer will be 'not many'.

I cannot emphasise enough how important this aspect is. Let's look at Mary, she has 4 direct reports who in turn have 10 people in each of their teams. Mary has been on all of the courses, done all of the self-study and she talks to her team about all of the things in this book. BUT does she turn up on time to all their 1 to 1s? Does she catch one of her team doing something well every day? Does she avoid favouritism? Does she turn her BlackBerry off in meetings? Is she 'visible'? Does she ignore 'non issues'?

If the answer to all of the above is yes – she Walks the Talk and engenders great respect amongst her team. If it's no to the odd one she will still be doing ok. If the answer to all is 'No' she has a parental attitude, 'Do what I say not what I do!'.

(Sorry to all parents, but as one myself, it is difficult, no impossible, not to do this occasionally with children. Children do live in a parallel universe and although I am sure some of the ideas in this book apply to looking after children I do not even pretend to understand where children come from so this guide is not intended for that purpose!)

Mary will not engender the amount of respect that she could by taking on board the suggestions in this book.

When I worked for a High Street Bank the highly respected MD (see 'Be seen') used to talk a lot about giving people responsibility and not operating in a blame culture, which was the overriding culture in the parent company. One day a tiny little error happened – the bank wrote to a large number of deceased customers. Once it had realised its error – due to a number of complaint calls from obviously distressed relatives, it wrote and apologised – to the deceased customers…

This was not a good marketing or publicity move and is rarely recommended in the 'How to boost sales' guides.

The MD got involved and the matter was dealt with. Retraining occurred where necessary, people were 'told off' for some pretty serious errors. End result was that everyone knew the consequences of their actions, some people lost end of year ratings over it, training and systems errors were highlighted and dealt with. Making the error once was bad, magnifying it with the follow up was appalling but not acting swiftly to block any further possible similar occurrence would have been unforgivable.

Issue dealt with. Then one of the two most senior executives in the Parent company got hold of the story. He immediately called the MD and said 'I want someone sacked'. The MD said that he had dealt with the situation - appropriate measures had been put into place and those responsible had been retrained or had their bonuses affected. The senior executive's blood pressure was rising 'I want names and I want sackings'. MD repeated his stance. 'You are not listening to me, I want blah blah blah'. The MD held his ground. This conversation was witnessed by a manager who happened to be in the office at the time. The news that the MD 'Walked the Talk' and would not submit to the pressure from on high for a sacrificial lamb went around the office of around 1,000 people like a bush telegraph. Respect? Maximum points.

End result? This particular matter would never happen again - in fact the company are probably the least likely company of their type to now accidentally write to dead customers. The MD preached certain values and he demonstrated them. No 'do as I say not as I do'. Just think about what had happened if he had given in and sacrificed a lamb. 'He might preach a certain culture, but when he's under pressure he's like all the others...' 'One rule for us and one rule for him...', 'Business culture? Don't make me laugh...', 'No blame culture unless he gets any blame of course...' And so on.

Be brave, ask your team what they think of you. 'Do they think you walk the talk?' There are many ways of obtaining upward feedback, 180 degree feedback, 360 degree feedback upward appraisals etc. that all add to a manager getting to know what his or her team think about how they manage. BUT that is process driven - what about creating a culture in your team where you can ask for feedback - and get it honestly.

One of the funniest upward feedback sessions I have been involved with saw us giving feedback on a particular boss anonymously. The idea/process was for the boss to discuss the overall findings with the team and agree ways forward in a non threatening and constructive way. Right…

Actually it involved, at high volume, 'Who said that? I demand to know who said that. If you think that you are wrong! We are not leaving here until I know who said what and you admit you are wrong!'

All I can say is that everyone got very familiar with their own shoes and the meeting ended quickly and in total silence. Good idea badly handled.

What do you have to lose? If they tell you what you already know you can't both be wrong. If they tell you something different it's an opportunity to put things right.

Anyway, be open and encourage (not demand) feedback. There are several guides and courses as to how to run an effective upward feedback session. One of the best is from The Richard Denny Group - www.denny.co.uk.

TIP If you are frightened of upward feedback - why? Do you know what they will say? If so why aren't you doing anything about it if things need to change?

Do you not know what they will say? Why? Aren't you communicating effectively, aren't you 'being aware', aren't you operating a culture that encourages openness?

By definition if you are frightened of the process - you have something to be frightened of. Managers who achieve the highest respect have nothing to fear from any form of upward feedback.

Respect from Above

So far this book has concentrated on gaining respect from your team. What about from your boss? How do you achieve respect from above? (The boss not the almighty). The principles are the same as for gaining respect from your team. **Communicate, Understand, Business Culture and Actions.**

Communicate – How does your boss like you to communicate? No point sending them copies of everything if they don't want it. Learn what they want and make sure you communicate with that in mind. Care – some bosses will say that they don't want to be copied in on everything and then criticise when they find out something from someone else. Learn actively and quickly!

Understand – What makes your boss tick? If it is working 25 hours a day fine but don't get sucked into following suit. What drives them? Is it a quest for personal glory? Is it a burning desire to help the company, promotion or just an easy life? Learn what it is and work with it. Make sure they know what your skills are and by using your abilities they can meet their goals. Are they a boss who needs to see everything and won't let go? If so make sure that you get everything accurate - suggest decisions, learn what makes them tick and align the way you present solutions.

Business Culture – difficult one this. If your boss is a real stickler for something that is really annoying and not company policy (e.g. everyone to wear white shirts) you need to communicate. Sometimes they will not waiver from some very long held beliefs. But - just because they stick to their guns doesn't mean that you have to follow suit (no pun intended). If they will only respect you for undying subservience try to evolve the culture, but you may need to move on. Try to create a culture in your team that you believe in and help them understand that there are some things it ain't worth fighting!

Actions - show your boss that you are a great manager. Great managers get results from their teams whether that is football, rugby, public sector work, industry or commerce. Show them that by sticking to your principles and applying some of the respect techniques in this book you achieve great things - it might rub off!

Overall? Your boss will want results. How do you achieve the best results? Ah that's by getting the best out of the team - see chapter 1, chapter 2, chapter 3...

TIP If you have a boss who is not interested in the 'hows' only the 'whats' do not let that rub off on you. Work with your team, gain their respect and that will achieve the results you strive for.

Self Assessment Quiz

As a bit of fun have a look through the questions below and give two answers.

The answer you would have given BEFORE reading this and...

The answer you would like to give AFTER reading this

Right. Let's go!

You are running late for a 1 to 1 with your team member. There is no way you can make it on time. Do you:

a) Just turn up late as usual.

b) Phone them to let them know so they don't waste time and cut the agenda to what you want to tell them.

c) As b) but give their agenda items priority.

It is the office Christmas party. You have had a very stressful time and want to let off some steam. Do you:

a) Get completely blasted and grope all around you equally so as not to show any favouritism or sexism.

b) Have a good few drinks and sit with the members of your team you like the most.

c) Take the car – stay as long as is appropriate, talk to all and drive (soberly) home. When home open wine and drink as long as you wish.

You need to mention to a member of staff that they will be going on a course in a couple of weeks time which will help their career prospects. Do you:

a) Make an appointment to see them via your secretary.

b) Wait for the monthly 1:1 that is due in a week's time.

c) Walk up to them as soon as you know and tell them all about it?

You haven't said anything to anyone in the team recently about jobs well done. You forgot that chapter of the book which is now in your bottom draw with old sandwich wrappings and several more unspeakable items. Do you:

a) Call your directs together and find out who has been doing what and who needs a thank you from the boss.

b) Do nothing as they will be suspicious of you being nice.

c) Refer to the HR manual under the 'what to do when someone does something well' section?

In your management of the team do you:

a) Make sure your team know that they should do as you coach them but not as you do yourself.

b) Always make sure you behave in a way that demonstrates your coaching.

c) Give neither approach a second thought as you are the boss so you do as you please.

The company have introduced a casual dress code. Do you:

a) Take on board and dress casually yourself.

b) Allow the team to take on board but maintain your own dress standards.

c) Make sure your team upholds the principles of business attire that are so dear to your heart.

You have an all day meeting that is over running. You know that one team member has a responsibility to an elderly relative and has to be away by 5.00. Do you:

a) Ignore the issue and hope that he/she would be too embarrassed to leave.

b) Make a very public announcement that Fred/Mary can't stay and all watch as they pack up and leave - hopefully feeling so embarrassed they won't mention it next time.

c) Have a quiet word in a tea break and say to them that they can slip out quietly at 5.00 and you will personally catch up with them the next day so that they don't miss anything.

You have a huge amount of work on and 3 employees give you their expenses (on time and correctly completed). You:

a) Put them to one side to sort out when you get 5 minutes

b) Make a special point of getting them done first thing in the morning.

c) Do them at the end of the month.

What percentage of your team's wives/ husbands/partners names do you know?

a) 100%.

b) 50%.

c) Who cares?

One of your team has done a great piece of work that qualifies for the company incentive scheme. Do you:

a) Fill in all the forms and keep it as a surprise.

b) Say thank you to the team member publicly and quickly, and set the wheels in motion for the incentive award.

c) Do nothing – isn't that what they are paid for?

A communication has been sent out by your team that shouldn't have gone. Do you:

a) Demand to know who sent it so you can tell the big bosses who it was.

b) Apologise, find out who it was and identify why – deal with those reasons appropriately.

c) Scream and shout propelling all toys well outside the pram.

A team member has a great record of completing a certain task on time and within budget. You are going on holiday – do you:

a) Make an exception due to your holiday that the team member can carry on without your sign off.

b) Insist that the sign off happens when you get back or that you interrupt your holiday to sign the job off from your BlackBerry whilst lying on the beach.

c) Let them carry on as normal – not needing your sign off.

Your company has great new ideas and visions about where they want to be in the future. Do you:

a) Share the ideas and vision with the team.

b) Not bother wasting time telling the team – the company are always changing it's 'vision' anyway.

c) Share ideas with the team and get their input as to how they can help you achieve the overall goal.

A mistake has happened in your team. Do you:

a) Make sure you find out who made the mistake so you can apportion blame and make sure the 'big bosses' know exactly who it was (and that it wasn't you).

b) Deal with the issues resulting from the error and put steps into place to rectify any individual or systems errors that caused it.

c) Pass the buck down the line to the most junior member possible (who will not be able to 'fight back').

You have to agree an important issue within the office which is causing some argument. Do you:

a) Write several emails to each other debating the points until agreement is reached.

b) Try to sneak an email on a cc basis when you know the others are busy.

c) Talk to the people concerned, agree actions and confirm by email.

You are running a meeting. One of the team (important but not essential to the meeting) is late. Do you?

a) Start on time – they can catch up.

b) Keep everyone waiting.

c) Abandon the meeting until another day.

One of your team tells you that a customer has complained about a decision they have made. Do you:

a) Discipline them for doing something that made the customer complain.

b) Tell them not to worry and ignore the customer who is a moaner anyway.

c) Thank them for raising the issue and work with them on a way to stop this type of complaint happening again.

You may wonder where are the answers? If you need the answers please go back to the beginning of this book...

Ok so this was a light hearted way to look back at some of the issues. BUT, (there is always a 'but') I guarantee that many managers actually think some of the less satisfactory answers are the right ones. Who has never heard of a manager who thinks that pay is all people need, who has worked for a manager who doesn't know any of his team's partner's names, who has had their expenses held up by a manager at some cost to themselves, who has seen a manager completely drunk at an office function making a complete fool of themselves, who has worked with parents of young children completely stressed by the pressure to work extra hours? I rest my case.

If you got all the answers right - genuinely - well done. My guess is that nearly 100% of managers will have a mixed set of answers, privately if not publicly. The figures from organisations such as the Institute of Leadership and Management and Investors in People would tend to support that.

If you take on board just one of the points mentioned in this book you WILL improve the respect your team has for you.

In Conclusion

Can you have the respect of your team without following the principles? Yes you can. There are some people who just have such strength of personality they get away with it. Having said that, you usually find that they do follow the principles in their own distinct way. 99% of managers need to follow a more traditional route to earning respect.

People skills do not come naturally to many people and often managers are promoted on technical or sales ability. Sometimes this does not make them natural leaders. These people have to work twice, no ten times, as hard to gain respect compared to those to whom it comes naturally. If you are a manager of managers it is your job to recruit properly and then to work with your managers to help them gain respect. You need to be looking at least one level below the people reporting to you. What effect is the manager having on them? Is he/she gaining their respect? If not what can you do about it? Do you Walk the Talk?

Don't forget where we started. The whole idea behind gaining respect is to make work lives better for you and your team and to maximise your efficiency. If your team respect you, you will gain output, credibility and probably personal progression - good managers are hard to find.

Respect lasts - think of bosses you have worked for. You will remember those who you respected with affection, your memory will conveniently forget the bad times under that boss. You will look back through rose coloured spectacles (or I guess contact lenses or laser surgery). That is the effect gaining respect has. What percentage of the bosses you have worked for did you genuinely respect? My guess is fairly low. It is hard to gain respect and anything that is worthwhile is often hard to achieve. Do you want to gain your team's respect?

Respect – if you expect it you might not get it. If you earn it, it will stay with you.

Thank you to three managers I have worked with for whom I have the utmost respect. They all saw a copy of this book in its early stages and I appreciated their feedback. Thanks to IC, JJ and MR – you know who you are!

Thank you to Richard Denny and team for their support and encouragement.

ALSO AVAILABLE FROM THE AUTHOR:

Training course

The 'Respect' programme is available as a two day course showing managers how to gain the respect of their teams. Pre course questionnaires are sent to the delegates teams to ascertain confidential information on what they think of their manager in terms of the respect they have for them. The questions are based around the sessions in the training programme.

During the programme there is a mixture of input from the trainer (the author of this book in many cases) real life situations experienced by the delegates and the anonymous feedback given by their teams.

The output is that the delegates much better understand what gains their teams respect and therefore leads to better productivity in a better working environment.

The programme can be tailored to junior managers just starting to manage teams to senior executives who manage large numbers of people or want the 'inside track' on working with their managers.

Presentation

The subject matter of this book is available from the author in presentation form. The presentation, which is suitable for all gatherings of managers of any seniority, is delivered around agreed areas of the 'Respect' subject. It takes a look at the simple actions that can increase respect while looking at some of the more obscure, but true, examples of actions that lose respect in an instant. Although dealing with a very serious subject the presentation is delivered with humour and encourages audience involvement.

The presentation is suitable for audiences of 10 to 1,000 and will challenge some long held beliefs. Delegates will leave thinking very hard about some aspects of how they manage their team.

MOTIVATIONAL/ INSPIRATIONAL BUSINESS BOOKS FROM DENNY PUBLISHING

Author Richard Denny will personalise and sign each copy of any of his international best sellers:

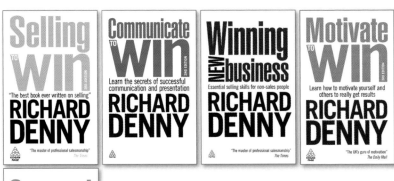

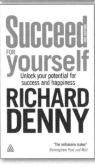

Three little books full of sayings
and quotes to stimulate and inspire!
Compiled by Richard Denny

Buy online at www.richarddenny.co.uk/shop

Richard Denny Presents Customer Care, Sales Training and Personal Attitude on DVD:

Customer Care - Complete Set of 3 DVDs or individual title available

Win a Sales 4 disc training course

Individual behavioural change

Buy online at: www.richarddenny.co.uk/shop

These audio CDs provide in-car motivational opportunities, turning unproductive time into valuable learning and personal development time.

Win More Sales

Sales techniques and inspiration which are really good common sense proved in practice. Ideal to learn about selling, or to recharge the batteries on those occasional gloomy days when sales have been difficult.

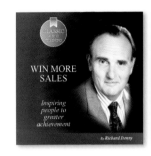

Dare to be Great

A personal development programme that helps you get more out of life as you deal with today's problems at work and at home. Use this programme to recognise the opportunities open to you and find out how to take them.

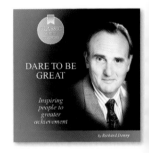

Motivational Management

Effective techniques for managers and others who lead people in teams or proects. This programme covers the great principles of management that so many forget. Play the CDs and have the confidence to motivate your people to greater achievement.

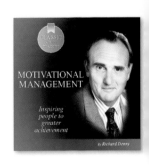

Buy online at: www.richardenny.co.uk/shop